Homesteading Animals (4)

Chunky Chickens For Meat & Eggs

By

Norman J Stone

Published By

www.deanburnpublications.com

Copyright Notice

Copyright © 2014, Norman J Stone

All rights reserved. Copyright protected. Duplicating, reprinting or distributing this material without the express written consent of the author is prohibited.

The information contained in this book is for general advice only. The statements contained herein have not been evaluated nor approved by the US Food & Drug administration.

While reasonable attempts have been made to assure the accuracy of the information contained within this publication, the author does not assume any responsibility for errors, omissions or contrary interpretation of this information, and any damages incurred by that.

The author does not assume any responsibility or liability whatsoever, for what you choose to do with this information.

The cooking and other techniques described in this publication are for your general guidance only.
Use your own judgment.

**

ISBN-13: 978-1500383206

2nd Print October 2014

Table of Contents

Contents

Introduction: *6*
Raising Chickens - Glossary of Terms *10*
Choosing Your Chickens: *14*
    Orpington 19
    The Light Sussex 20
    White Leghorn 21
    Plymouth Rock 23
    Welsummer Chicken 24
    Jersey Giant 25
    The Dorking 27
    Araucana 28
    Brahma 29
    Bantams 30
Chicken Coops *33*
    Coop V's Tractor 37
    The Chicken Run: 42
    Chicken Hut: 44
    Keeping Chickens Indoors: 46
Chicken Ailments: *50*
    Chicken Feed: 53
Processing Chickens for Meat: *56*

Dispatching the Chicken: 58
Removing The Feathers: 60
Cleaning & Dressing The Bird: 62

Tasty Chicken Recipes! 65

Chicken Breast With Parma Ham, Honey & Herbs 65
Spicy Chicken Casserole (2) 66
Honey Glazed Roast Chicken 67
Jamaican Jerk Chicken 68
Chicken & Smoked Ham Stew 69
Spatchcocked Chicken Stew 70
Fried Chicken With Lemon & Ginger 71
Spicy Chicken Burgers 72
Traditional Coq au Vin 73
Herby Chicken Breasts Stuffed With Cream Cheese & Prunes 74

Authors Note: 76

Books In The Homesteading Animals Series:

Homesteading Animals – Rearing Rabbits (book 1)

Homesteading Animals – Delightful Ducks (book 2)

Homesteading Animals: Gourmet Geese (book 3)

Homesteading Animals: Raising Chickens (book 4)

Introduction:

The sight of chickens scratching around the yard always lifts my heart a little, there is just something 'natural' about the scene that calms the spirit and assures me that all is well in the world.

Ok, I'll forgive you for thinking that I'm some kind of an idealist nutter! Anyhoo… rest assured, this book is all about the practical aspect of keeping chickens and why if you are not already doing so, you should seriously consider it if you have any free space at all.

The topics I will cover in this book include..

Chicken Choices:

What are your options regarding chicken breeds? How to choose your hens for either their ability to produce a good plump carcass; as well as how to choose the best birds for eggs – including production numbers and color.

Pictures and descriptions of a selection of the most popular chicken breeds.

Chicken Care:

Knowing how to properly care for your chickens is absolutely essential not only to get the best results out of them, but also for the birds sake. The chicken is going to give out much, and expect little in return apart from food, water and care – you owe it to them to do that; after all it is for your mutual benefit!

Chicken Coops:

What to look for in a chicken coop and how to protect your chickens from the designs of predators. How to set up perches and nest boxes; as well as general information on keeping your coop (as well as your birds) disease free.

Dispatching & Dressing Your Birds:
If you are rearing your chickens for meat then you will have to know how to dispatch the bird. Here I will show the best ways to kill the bird cleanly and humanely as well as the easiest ways to pluck the chicken and prepare it for the table.

Selection of Recipes:
This work would not be complete without a selection of good chicken recipes! Here I have some of the best recipes courtesy of F. A. Paris who has kindly given me permission to include ten tasty recipes from the 'Fantastic Chicken' cookbook.

Chicken Care Glossary:
There is also a glossary of the popular terms used when dealing with chickens. This is a handy go-to resource and includes a brief description.

Other Chicken Benefits:
Everyone is aware of the benefits of keeping chickens, especially where eggs and meat are concerned. I would hazard a guess in fact, that the chicken is perhaps the most popular domestic bird on the planet!
However apart from eggs and meat, the chicken has other attributes well worth considering.

Recycling!

Yes, this humble bird is an excellent natural recycler of just about anything organic! It will happily eat your kitchen vegetable cuttings, as well as scraps of meat and other cooked food. Next to the pig, I rate it as the top natural food-garbage disposal unit!

Compost Booster:
Chicken manure is an excellent source of nitrogen – a top component in any good fertilizer. Some well-rotted chicken manure added to your compost will assure you of a great harvest from your veggie patch.

Use sparingly though, and only on manure that has rotted for over 1 year, otherwise it is just too nitrogen-rich for many plants to cope with.

Pest Control:
Chickens are excellent at controlling pests as they will happily munch away at just about anything that creeps or crawls. In fact I have even witnessed them chasing and eating mice that wander into their path.

Put a couple of chickens into your vegetable patch <u>before</u> you plant your spring veggies, and they will peck away at any surface bugs, as well as scrape up any ground-dwellers such as the cut-worm and other grubs that otherwise will creep out and destroy your veggies.

You can help them out here by forking over the ground to expose the bugs – your hens will love you for it!

Companionship:

Yes you may well laugh! However it has been shown by countless studies, that caring for any animal can be very beneficial for your mental health.

The fact is that some chickens like the Rhode Island Red, do in fact make very good pets, and will follow you around just like a dog! This of course is great - unless you intend eating it!

A word of warning in this respect – never name an animal you are planning to eat (unless your name is Hannibal Lecter!). It is just not natural to kill a friend, and if you name an animal it becomes your friend in some strange anthropomorphic way.

With all that said, let's get down to business and discover the world of raising chickens…

Raising Chickens - Glossary of Terms
Some terms to familiarize yourself with

Bantam: This small bird is about half the size of the normal chicken, and is normally bred for ornamental purposes. Many chicken varieties have a bantam equivalent.

Bedding: Bedding for chickens usually consists of shavings, sawdust or straw. This is placed under the perches in particular and is used to absorb and collect the droppings. Bedding is also placed within the nest boxes to protect the eggs from breakage, as well as to help keep them clean.

Broody Hen: This is a hen that has settled down to 'brood' or to hatch out a clutch of eggs. Broody hens should be set aside and kept in a quiet nest-box with a few artificial eggs under them, if you do not intend hatching eggs.

Broiler: A chicken especially bred for commercial meat production.

Candling: A candle is held up to the egg to enable the light to shine through and determine whether or not it has been fertilized or not. This is used if you are separating eggs to be hatched out at a later date – perhaps fertilized eggs you may want to sell.

Capon: This is a rooster that has been castrated usually to add weight when rearing the bird for the Christmas table for instance.

Clutch: A number of eggs gathered to hatch out under a broody hen.

Cockerel: A male chicken.

Comb: This is the red floppy ridge over the top of the chickens head. This is more prominent in the cockerel or rooster. It can also be a good indicator of the birds general health.

Coop: This is a general term for the chicken shed.

Crop: A chicken deposits it's food into a pouch in the esophagus, before it is transferred to the stomach.

Droppings Tray: This is a tray that can be located under the chicken perches for quick removal.

Dust bath: This is an area set aside where the chicken can 'bath' in dust, in order to release dry skin, mites and any other detrimental insects.

Feeder: Something to hold and deliver the food pellets for feeding the hens.

Fertilized egg: This is an egg from a chicken that has been mated with a rooster, resulting in fertilization.

Grain Scratch: This is a selection of grains scattered on the ground for the chickens to scratch and peck at. This keeps the chicken busy and deters anti-social behavior such as pecking at other birds.

Grit Bins: Birds need grit in their diet in order to aid digestion and help create strong egg-shells. Particularly important if your chickens do not get to scratch in the dirt.

Hackles: This is the neck feathers of the chicken.

Hen: Female chicken.

Incubation: This is the period where the egg is being heated by natural or artificial means in order to promote growth of the embryo in the egg:

Incubator: Artificial equipment for hatching out eggs. Can also refer to a broody hen.

Layer feed: This is food that has been prepared especially for laying hens.

The Molt: This usually happens about once a year, and is a process whereby the hen will shed its feathers to grow new ones. Laying is suspended while hens are going through the molt.

Nest box: A box provided where the chickens can lay their eggs. Usually 1 box is provided to serve 3-4 hens.

Point-of-lay Chicken: This describes a bird around 22-24 weeks of age – just before it begins to lay its first egg.

Production breeds: These are breeds of chickens used for the mass-production of eggs.

Pullet: A young chicken not yet at laying age.

Roost: This is the place (or the perches) where the chickens sleep for the night.

Rooster: Mature male chicken.

Roosting pole: A perch put in place for the chickens to roost at night.

Run: A fenced in area where the chickens can roam.

Sexing: Determining the sex of the bird.

Shanks: The bottom part of the chickens legs.

Spur: This is a sharp protrusion at the foot of the Roosters used for fighting with other males.

Started pullet: Similar to the point-of-lay pullet, but this one has started to lay its first eggs.

Starter feed: A special food formulated to encourage growth of young chickens.

Vent: Similar to the anus of other animals, the vent however is also where the eggs are produced in chickens and other fowl.

Wattles: This is red and rubbery similar to the comb, but it is situated under the chickens neck.

Wheezer: Slang name for the chickens rear-end.

Wormer: Treatment for the removal of worms from the animals intestinal tract.

Choosing Your Chickens:

No-one knows quite how many breeds of chickens there are in the world today, but to say it is in the hundreds would be no exaggeration. The good news however is that you don't have to be able to name them all!

Before you rush out and buy your chickens, there are some important things you may want to consider, such as..

1. Your Requirements:
Are you thinking of keeping chickens for their eggs or their meat, or indeed both? This is an important question because different breeds will produce eggs or meat in diverse quantities.

If you are intending keeping your chickens for eggs only then you would choose a good layer such as the White Leghorn, which is one of the exceptional egg-layers producing around 300 eggs per annum.

The Jersey Giant on the other hand is a fantastic bird for the table as it weighs in at around 14 lbs when full grown. As you may expect it is much slower on the egg production, however this giant bird does produce an above-average sized egg!

2. Local Considerations:
Consider the breeds that are more prevalent in your immediate area; these are usually the tried-and-tested varieties that have been chosen for generations owing to their ability to thrive in your local conditions.

Don't be afraid to experiment however with different breeds – just be sure you have checked up on their ability to cope with your local climate in particular.

3. Breeding?
Are you considering rearing chickens from your own hens? In this case you will need to keep a Rooster handy to do the business!

If you do not intend breeding home-grown chic's, then I would forego the Rooster as it will only be detrimental to the egg-laying chickens.

Another thing to consider is local regulations – they can be quite strict when it comes Roosters in particular as the cock-crowing in the early hours tends to upset some neighbors.

4. Chicks or Chickens?
When deciding to keep chickens you have first of all to consider what age to buy them at. You can purchase day-old chicks for only few dollars each, but you have to be prepared to keep them under a heat lamp while they grow their feathers.
You must also be prepared for some mortality – more so if you are new to the idea of raising chicks.

As the age of the chicks goes up then so does the price, with the most expensive being point-of-lay pullets costing around $25-$30 each. This is to be compared with the cost of day-old chicks at around $3 each.

However, before you think of the huge price difference and jump at the day-old option – consider the cost and labour as well as the possible mortality rate of the growing chicks over a 5-6 month period.

Your costs should include the price of the chicks, plus the cost of starter chicken meal. The cost of construction or purchasing a heated facility for them, as well as the electric costs for keeping a heating lamp running 24/7.

5. Ornamental:
Maybe you are not too fussy regarding your hens, or indeed are just looking for a bird to add some color and activity to your yard? In this case you can choose to keep bantam hens from many breeds, that will add some real color and be a great talking point as they scrape around the yard.

Not entirely without practical use, these little birds will still produce a small egg, and will still eat and poop – giving you a ready supply of manure for your composting!

Top Chicken Choices

Rhode Island Red

This is probably one of the most popular chickens around, and not without good cause. It is an excellent layer – producing 5-7 eggs per week, and it is a hardy bird able to withstand a wide range of climatic conditions.

It is a popular choice as an all-round bird as it is also a good choice as a meat bird, and they also make great pets! One of the characteristics of this bird is that it will form an attachment to its owner and will follow them around like a pet dog.

The Rooster however can be quite territorial, and it is not unknown for one to actually chase away some much larger and more dangerous predators like the fox or even stoat!

An excellent choice of bird for the beginner, as it needs little care in order to produce the goods.

The Rhode Island Red is also the state bird of Rhode Island in New England.

***

Orpington

Originally bred in Orpington England, this is another popular bird mainly chosen for its eggs. It has a good calm nature and is not easily flustered, even by the pet dog or children!

Full grown the hen weighs in at 8-10 lbs. It is a good layer and produces a large brown egg. Perfect for a backyard bird, it does not fly much and is able to withstand cold climates owing to its large bulk.

The **Buff Orpington** is also a popular choice and as the name suggests is light-tan in color.

***

The Light Sussex

Known as a duel-purpose bird the Sussex is a breed renowned for its tasty meat as well as producing up to 260 good sized, light brown eggs over the year. It is also a sociable bird and good with children, able to thrive in open spaces or within smaller enclosures.

There are several different colors of this bird, but the most popular are the light, buff and silver varieties.

***

White Leghorn

The Leghorn was originally bred in Tuscany, central Italy. This bird is an excellent layer producing up to 300 white eggs per year.

This bird is not considered as a viable meat bird as it weighs in fully grown at around 4.5lbs.

It tends to be a nervous and rather flighty bird that is not comfortable in human company, and should definitely be kept well away from the family pets.

This bird comes in many different colors, perhaps the most popular next to the White is the Brown Leghorn, although this does not lay as many eggs as the white..

***

Plymouth Rock

Often referred to as the Barred Rock, this is an impressive bird weighing in at around 8 lbs when full grown. It is also a very productive egg-layer and for this reason is regarded as dual-purpose bird good for eggs and meat.

It has a calm nature and gets along very well alongside humans and pets. Eight distinct colors are recognized worldwide. Barred, White, Buff, Partridge, Silver Penciled, Blue, Columbian, and Black.

It lays a medium sized light brown egg.

***

Welsummer Chicken

This is a popular bird that lays an attractive large dark brown egg, often with darker spots speckled on the surface. Weighing-in at around 6lbs it is not considered to be commercially suitable for meat production, and as such is largely reared for the eggs – though it is considered to be a moderate egg-layer producing around 180-200 eggs per year.

Bred from a combination of Rhode Island Reds, Barnevelders, Partridge Leghorns, Cochins, and Wyandotte's; the Welsummer is a friendly breed although perhaps a bit flighty, and will follow its owner around like a pet.

***

Jersey Giant

As the name suggests, this is indeed a giant of a bird – originally bred to replace the domestic turkey – whilst the mature hen weighs in at over 10lbs, the Rooster can reach 13lbs and more.

Needless to say this bird is primarily bred for its meat, although it does produce around 180 large brown eggs over the year.

It is a docile bird and very hardly in colder conditions. It is also considered to be an excellent choice for winter eggs, which it will produce happily if sheltered from the worst conditions.

***

The Dorking

Considered to have been exported by the Romans into Britain around the time of the Roman conquest; this is considered to be a dual purpose bird in that it reaches a reasonable weight of around 7lb for the Hen (9lb for the Rooster), and is also a good layer producing over 200 white-shelled eggs per year.

It is a quiet docile bird and easy to manage, making it ideal for the backyard chicken. There are 5 recognized varieties of the Dorking - White, Silver-grey, Red, Dark and Cuckoo.

The picture above shows an impressive silver-grey Rooster, with the smaller hens in the background.

***

Araucana

Also known as the South American Rumpless, this unusual bird has no tail-head (hence the name) and has little tufts of feathers growing out the side of its neck. It is considered a dual purpose bird in that it has a good well-fleshed out carcass, and produces over 200 blue colored eggs per year.

It is often confused with the Ameraucana chicken, which also produces a blue egg, but has a full tail and is a slightly heavier bird.

Thought to have been first bred by the Araucanian Indians of Chile; they come in several colors including Black, White, Black Breasted Red, Blue, Buff, and Silver.

***

Brahma

Developed in America from birds imported from Shanghai in the early 1850's, the Brahma is a large docile bird, generally reared for its meat owing to its size (Hen around 9.5lb, Rooster 12lb).

However it is considered a good winter layer as it is able to withstand the cold and produce a good number of large brown eggs.

They come in a wide range of colors apart from the light, dark and buff that you see in the above picture.

***

Bantams

Whilst a true Bantam has no larger counter-part, the term 'Bantam' is generally used to describe any small chicken breed that has been developed from the larger full-size chicken.

They are mainly bred for show purposes, or just for their attractive qualities as they scrape around the yard. However their diminutive size means that they are an attractive option for anyone looking for chickens in a smaller yard.

Many Bantam breeds like the Brahma make excellent pets as they seem to love human company. They will also produce up to 100 or so small eggs per year (about a third the size of a grade A chicken egg), as well as scrape around eating up pests and bugs around the yard.

The Silkie as in the following picture, is a very popular breed for showing.

Consideration has to be taken regarding their protection, as they are particularly vulnerable to a large range of predators.

Family pets as well as the Fox, Badger, Coyote, Raccoons etc will all love to snack on your Bantams. Smaller predators like the Mink, Stoat and Weasel – as well as many raptors and snakes, have to be kept well away from your tiny birds if they are to survive.

Most of these predators are of course a threat to your larger chickens also, however the Bantam is just that bit more vulnerable – who say's size doesn't matter!

Chicken Coops

Even free-range chickens must have a coop (or chicken shed). This is an essential requirement for their protection from predators as well as from the weather; and for a place where they can lay their eggs – otherwise (in the case of free-range) you will be collecting eggs from under every bush and hiding place.

Left to their own devices it's quite amazing where chickens will wander to find that perfect place for laying, usually somewhere you will discover many days or even weeks afterwards!

With that in mind, here are some construction tips and things to consider, regarding chicken coops and nesting boxes.

Living Space

Every living thing needs a certain space in order to prosper, and chickens are of course no exception. General rules vary of course when it comes to space requirements in a coop where they will roost only, compared to the space needed in a chicken run where they will scratch around and do what chickens do!

With regard to a perch where they will rest for the night. A chicken only needs about 12 inches of space per chicken (9 inches for Bantam breeds), with a minimum of 18 inches head-room. This is simply so that they do not bump their heads when flying up on to the perch.

Floor space in a coop or shed has to be at least 3-4 square feet per chicken, whilst the space in the run should be around 10 square foot per bird.

At this point it is worth considering that a 'Free Range' bird according to DEFRA only has to have *"...had during at least half [it's] lifetime continuous daytime access to open-air runs, comprising an area mainly covered by vegetation, of not less than: $1m^2$ per chicken."*

I consider this space allocation quite mean however - Why is this worth considering? You **can sell free range eggs** for a lot more money!

Perches themselves can be made from 4 x 2 timbers with the top edges rounded off, and around 18 inches between chickens. If several chickens are to be house then a stepped design as in the picture below is ideal for the job.

As you can see, the hens can sit quite happily as the 2 inch wide beam offers just the right amount of support.

The area beneath the perches has to be accessible for regular clean-up, especially as this is where the most poop will gather. This is generally done at least once per week.

Nest Boxes do not have to be complicated, a simple space giving around 12 inches for the bird to sit will suffice just fine.
This can be in the form of a wooden box structure, or perhaps a simple space with areas sectioned off into compartments as in the picture below.
The main thing is that the birds have peace to lay and are not disturbed. A frightened bird is likely to break eggs and be put off laying altogether.

At least 1 box or nesting space is required for every 3-4 birds, otherwise they will struggle for space which will result in broken eggs. On another issue. The last thing you want is to leave broken eggs lying around – this will result in the birds eating the broken eggs, and developing a taste for them.

Birds that do this will often later break them deliberately to eat! Remove broken eggs immediately to avoid this happening.

Back to the nest boxes. Finally put some soft material like hay, straw, shavings or even shredded newspaper into the box to help prevent breakages and encourage the bird to use it.

Coop V's Tractor

There are two main structures when it comes to housing your chickens, and these are the coop and the tractor – often referred to in the same breath.

Tractors tend to be light-weight triangular structures suitable for large spaces where they can be moved around, where permanent coops tend to be more robust, larger and suitable where space is limited.

There is however one main difference between the two chicken houses, and that is that the 'tractor' is generally thought of as a mobile coop with a small 'run' or enclosed space attached.

This comes in many shapes and sizes but is basically a small 'run' enclosed with chicken wire, and with a shelter and nest-box at one end. This can be lifted by means of handles like a wheelbarrow and wheeled around to fresh pasture daily.

The tractor has several advantages & disadvantages when compared with the static coop design.

Tractor - Advantages:
1. Chickens are constantly grazing on fresh pasture which means that the ground is not becoming infested with mites and disease.

2. Scratching around in the grass or even dirt, is good for the chickens digestion and should ensure a regular diet of essential grit.

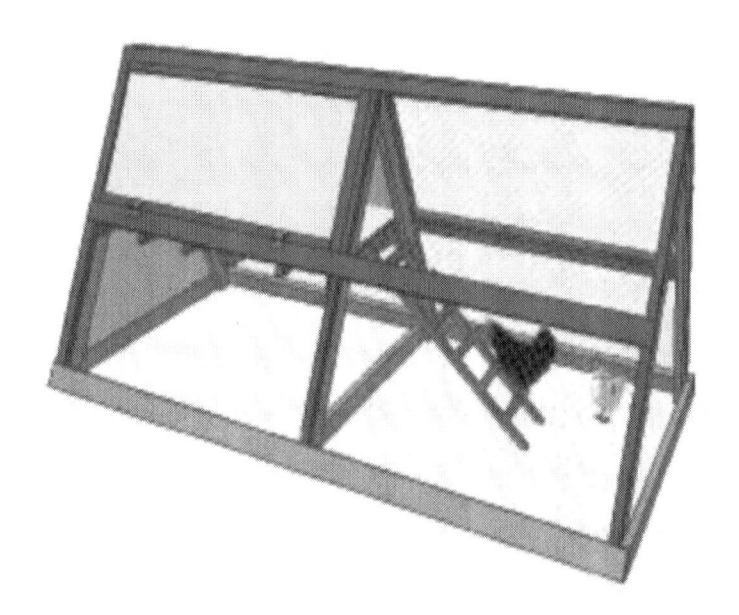

With this design simply add wheels and handles to make it more mobile.

3. A busy chicken is a happy chicken, and a happy chicken lays more eggs!

4. Free fertilizer! Chicken poop is rich in nitrogen, which your grass loves. Not only that the chickens scratching around in the grass will eat up the bugs and grubs as well as aerate the grass.

5. Less maintenance! By this I mean cleaning out, as your chickens will mainly poop in the grass and not the small shelter and nest box attached.

Tractor - Disadvantages:
1. It can be a royal pain having to move the tractor every day – especially if the weather is bad!

2. Since the idea is that the tractor is mobile, it is usually quite small – allowing only a few birds.

3. The structure of the mobile tractor is fairly light and consequently flimsy. This means that strong predators can more easily gain access to your precious chickens.

4. Unless you have a large enough area to move it around on a daily basis, the yard will soon become foul and messy.

Permanent Coop – Advantages:
1. A permanent design can be made to any size, so you are not restricted to the number of chickens you can keep.

2. Easy to hook up to water and electric supplies – especially important for lighting to encourage winter laying birds.

3. It can be a more robust structure to keep at bay predators like foxes or coyotes, big cats etc.

4. A permanent coop takes up less space, being a fixed structure; and is easier to keep warm and weatherproof especially over cold winters.

Permanent Coop Disadvantages:

1. Maintenance or cleaning has to be carried out on a more frequent basis, otherwise parasites and disease will infest the coop. Also the smell will upset neighbors and attract vermin.

2. The chickens will have to be closed up every night (unless in a fully enclosed run) to protect them from predators.

Typical Store-Bought Small Permanent Coop

3. A permanent structure is generally more expensive to build than a tractor as it will require more lumber and other materials. Store-bought permanent coops are also more expensive to buy than the tractor versions.

4. Because they are set in the same place, the ground area of the run will soon become a waste-land and in danger of going foul and infested.

Summary:

As you can see, there is a lot to consider before you house your chickens! However according to your particular circumstances, each style will have its merits and the decision over which to employ can only be taken after everything is properly considered.

The Chicken Run:

The chicken 'run' is simply the enclosed structure that is attached to your coop – that is unless the birds are allowed to roam free.

Most birds though even if they are free-range, have some kind of enclosure where they can be closed in occasionally and protected against predators, and it is always advisable to lock up your chickens in an enclosed coop overnight.

The run itself is a frame-work usually made from lumber of a robust nature (min 2 x 2), and is covered by chicken mesh with no more than 1" holes otherwise small predators such as stoats and weasels, snakes etc will gain entry.

On permanent structures, the mesh should be taken a minimum of 6 inches into the ground, with 3-4 inches at the bottom turned toward you as per the diagram.

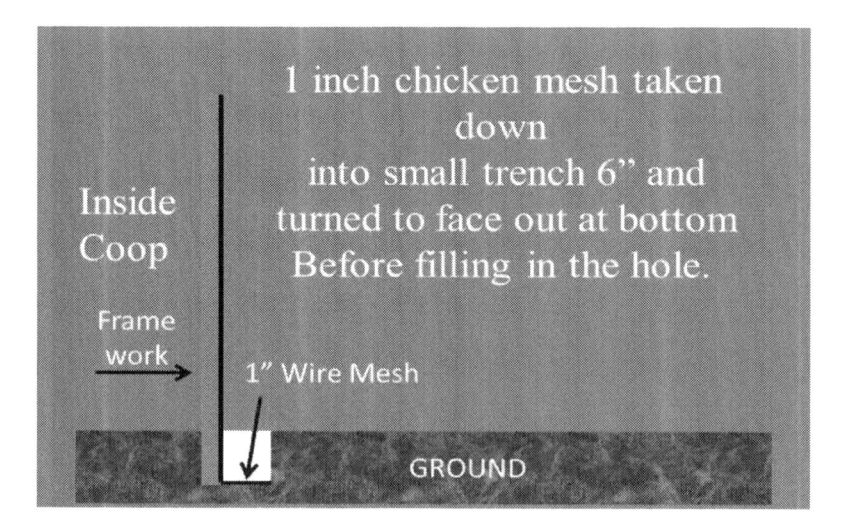

This will prevent determined diggers from digging down and under the mesh, as when they reach the bottom they will encounter more wire!

On the subject of determined predators – if you are in an area where the fox, coyote, or badger or stray dogs etc are likely to be hunting, then the addition of 2" weld mesh will be needed at least on the lower 3 foot of the frame-work.

Any one of these critters will make short work of chicken mesh if they are hungry enough.

As for the roof of the run itself; I prefer to cover this over rather than keep it open or covered with mesh. The reason is that a covered run keeps the area below at least partially dry, which prevents it from becoming a wet, stinking pest-trap!

Chicken Hut:

The hut for locking up your chickens and collecting the eggs, can come in many shapes and sizes – one such store-bought example has already been shown in the earlier picture.

This is a typical example with a nest box that can be accessed from the outside, meaning that you do not have to go into the shed at all except to perform duties such as cleaning-out, tending to birds etc.

However a simple garden shed can do for a chicken coop, just cut in a small access door about 12 inches square for access.

If the shed is raised from the ground, then provide a simple ramp to access the coop as in the example below. This particular example allows the chickens access to a raised area within the shed.

Apart from areas for roosting and nesting – as explained in previous chapters – it is imperative that there is adequate provision for ventilation and general activities.

As a general rule, a chicken hut must have around 4 square feet of floor space per bird. This is not to be confused with the space needed for a chicken run or indeed for keeping chickens in deep-litter (see later chapter). In these situations at least 10 square foot <u>of floor space</u> per bird is required.

The reasons for this are simple. Apart from allowing individual birds their own space for scratching around and keeping busy, it also helps prevent bullying and reduces respiratory problems amongst the birds.

This is also an important aspect of adequate ventilation. If the coop is not properly vented especially in hot or humid conditions, then respiratory problems are likely to arise – leading to sickly and under-performing birds.

Always bear in mind that a chicken stressed-out or unhappy in any way will show you how she feels by reduced egg-laying or stopping production all together!

Keeping Chickens Indoors:

The alternative method of housing chickens is to keep them indoors permanently. This is not to be confused with the 'battery' method of intensive chicken farming, but is a very effective way of keeping happy healthy chickens that will produce eggs all-year round.

This is because they are warm – even over winter - well fed and safe from predators; the perfect combination for great results.

Introducing The Deep Litter Method:
If you have a large shed or barn, preferably with a dirt floor, then this is ideal for keeping hens indoors using what is called the deep litter method.

This system means very little maintenance with regard to 'mucking out' and is perhaps the simplest method of raising healthy productive birds.

The general idea of deep litter is that you allow the litter to build up over a period of time, just adding more pine shavings when necessary to freshen it up a bit.

Although you might think that this will lead to unhygienic conditions, the exact opposite is the case. In a good dry indoor environment, this means that the litter heats up slightly helping to warm the coop and keep fly's and parasites at bay.

In a properly run deep litter coop, smells and flies should be at an absolute minimum, and performance with regard to egg-laying is maximized as the chickens are scratching around in the shavings and generally having a great time!

Setting up your deep litter coop:
First of all make sure that your barn or shed floor is dry, and that there are no leaks in the roof. This is important as wet litter will lead to smells and poor conditions in the coop.

After you have laid out a suitable roosting area at one end of your shed, and sorted out nest boxes as per the previous chapters; cover the floor area with about 6 inches of fresh pine shavings.

For a deep litter coop a dirt floor is preferable, as it allows for drainage and dust-bathing; but if it is already concreted over then this will do adequately.

Hang up suitable water dispensers and lay out your food pellet feeders as normal. Make sure particularly with the water dispensers that the chickens are not able to knock them over. If the chickens have access to the outdoors, then keep the water feeders outside.

There are numerous store-bought choices for these water and food dispensers that will do the job just fine.

Maintenance:
Maintaining the litter could not be easier. Simply clean out the worst of the muck under the roost every month or so, replacing with fresh shavings. As for the rest of the floor area; turn over with a fork if you see it getting compacted at all, the chickens will love this and will soon muck-in to lend a hand!

Give your coop a good clear out spring and fall. Adding the litter to the compost heap and leaving to rot for a further year or so, makes excellent nitrogen-rich compost for the vegetable patch.

Top Tips:
Add a few handfuls of food-grade diatomaceous earth to the litter every now and then. This is a natural product that is harmless to animals and humans, but is an effective killer of mites and other parasites.

Hang up a few cabbages or swedes or bunches of vegetable matter at head height in the shed. This will keep the chickens active especially if they have no access to an outside area. This is important in order to stop them getting bored and pecking each other.

Scatter a few handfuls of whole barley or other scratching onto the litter to keep them busy and happy.

Proper ventilation is especially important in a closed-in chicken hut. Make sure that you have vents at eaves height, and some just above floor level to encourage a good flow of air. Be careful however that they do not get a cold draft, especially where they roost at night.

I prefer to have an open mesh-covered window area that I leave open at all times except during the harshest or coldest weather.

Dust Bath:
This is more needed if the floor of your shed is concrete or some such material. If this is the case then provide a shallow container about two feet square and 6 inches deep filled with dry sand.

Chickens love to have a dust bath as it helps remove mites and other parasites. A handful (not too much) of food-grade Diatomaceous earth in it will discourage any resident parasites.

Winter Laying:
During the shorter daylight hours of winter keep a light on in the shed so that the hens are subjected to at least 14 hours 'daylight' per day. Any shorter than this and the egg-laying will slow down considerably.

Summary:
In short, the deep litter method is my favorite choice for keeping chickens for all of the reasons mentioned.

However I am fortunate enough to have a decent sized barn that houses two dozen chickens. The result is a good regular egg supply from happy contented chickens – with very little effort on my part!

Chicken Ailments:

Generally speaking, if chickens are kept well fed and watered in conditions similar to those just gone over, then disease or parasites is not something that should cause undue concern.

Personally I have suffered very little over the years with any of the parasites or ailment listed below, not because I am some sort of hot-shot animal carer, but just because I have followed the basic rules of care. That said however 'stuff' happens as they say.

The usual symptoms of chicken mite or lice infestation on your birds are things like, general listlessness, loss of appetite, poor laying, pale combs, bald spots, scabs and general poor condition of feathers.

Anyhow, that said, there are certain ailments that any chicken keeper would be wise to at least know about, just in case they should rear their ugly head. Here is a short-list of the most common of them.

1. Chicken Mites:
The Northern Fowl Mite and the Red Roost Mites are the most prevalent of the many mite species likely to bother your birds. They are blood-feeders and come in many colors from yellowish-brown to bright red. They come out at night to feed on the poor chicken as it roosts.

During daytime they hide in crevasses and cracks in nest-boxes and on perches. Tiny creatures not visible to the human eye, they are evident only by the symptoms already mentioned.

Treatment involves applying a product such as Sevin Dust to the roosts and nest boxes as well as to the birds.

Eprinex is a liquid treatment that is also very effective and should be applied to the same areas.

A wood ash dust bath is a very effective and 'natural' treatment against many parasites.

Neem oil sprayed on the perches and nest boxes will kill of any parasites hiding out during daytime.

Scaly Leg Mite:
This mite attacks the feet and legs of the bird and separates the scales from the living flesh – leaving the legs tender and sore.
Petroleum jelly, linseed oil or vegetable oil gently rubbed into the leg for a week or so will usually solve the problem.

Poultry Lice:
These critters feed on the dry skin and feathers of the chicken, causing irritation and feather loss as the bird pulls out its feathers. Poor egg production and listlessness are other signs of louse infestation.

A check around the vent area of an infested bird will reveal these parasites that unlike Mites, are visible to the human eye. Clusters of eggs stuck to the base of the feathers and lice hanging around the area is proof of infestation.

General:

As is usually the case, prevention is easier than the cure in many instances. Keeping your coops clean by performing regular inspections, and washing down perches and boxes with the appropriate treatment s like Neem Oil for instance, will prevent possible infestation from gaining any foothold.

Keep a pair of boots handy near or inside the coop, and only wear these when you are entering the coop itself. Many diseases are transferred from outside on boots that have picked it up elsewhere. Also, <u>Never</u> wear the same boots (unless disinfected beforehand) when visiting other coops for fear of disease transfer.

As a precaution, <u>never</u> introduce new birds to your flock without giving them a thorough inspection for signs of lice or mites. In fact I always keep new birds separate for at least 1 week before re-inspecting them and introducing them to the flock if they are still ok.

By taking these simple precautions you will prevent major hassle later on if Mites or lice do manage to get established.

Chicken Feed:

Bear in mind that chickens are omnivores – meaning that they will eat, or attempt to eat, almost anything! I've seen a chicken catch and pick up a mouse by the tail, then be chased all over the run by the others who wanted a piece of the action.

They will eat all kinds of veggies and seeds, and in their scratching around will consume a vast number of bugs and critters. However although they *will* eat almost anything, that does not mean to say that they *should e*at almost anything.

However let's begin at the beginning, as through their growth stage their diet differs.

Chicks:
For the first 24 hours a chic is sustained by the egg-sac that is still inside it. Thereafter it should be fed a fine ground meal such as a chicken-starter meal which is only around 18% protein.

If you intend to slaughter the bird for meat, then a special **chicken growth feed** is an option, otherwise feed the chicks the starter feed for about the first 14 weeks or so.

Always make sure there is plenty of **clean** water nearby, especially as the fine meal needs something to wash it down! The water in the dispenser can soon become clogged and contaminated with the meal, so this has to be cleaned out regularly.

Consider using a water dispenser with bleed nipples, as this will keep the water clear from meal contamination.

Pullets:

At around 16 weeks a chicken is known as a point-of-lay bird, and as the name suggests it is soon to enter the ranks of laying chickens and contribute to the homestead economy!

While not absolutely necessary (despite what the feed manufacturers would say) you can feed the young hens on a special pullet developer pellet, that has just the right amount of nutrients for this stage in their growth.

A clean, regular supply of water is of course essential during all stages of the hens life cycle.

Laying Hens:

A hen will become fully productive at around 6 months or earlier according to the breed. Laying eggs on a daily basis is a depleting business for hens, and the feed must have enough nutrients, calcium and minerals to make up for the daily loss through egg production.

It does of course vary by the breed, but a standard size adult chicken will eat around 6 oz of chicken pellets per day. In order to keep the bird in top health however, it is good to add to this a selection of mixed greens to peck at, along with some scratching's on the floor to keep them active.

The addition of some grit in a box with oyster shell, will ensure good digestion and a strong egg-shell, and some treats like a handful of sunflower seeds will be gratefully received by your chickens.

Watering your chickens is simply a question of providing plenty of clean water daily – an average adult hen will consume almost a pint of water per day - A chicken without water will expire within a day especially in warm conditions.

Water containers are best hung from the roof or placed off the ground on bricks, to prevent the water becoming contaminated with food and muck.

What <u>Not</u> to Feed Chickens:
As mentioned at the beginning of this chapter, chickens will eat or attempt to eat almost anything you offer them. However there are certain foods you should avoid giving them as they are likely to cause harm in one form or another.

Let's be real about this though – we all eat stuff that is not good for us, but usually in moderation, it is unlikely to do us any real harm. The same can be said for your chickens. An odd bit of chocolate or a few sunflower seeds will not do any harm, but given all the time will lead to digestion and other problems – similar to what you could have if you eat burgers every day!

With that said however, here is a short list of foods that you should definitely avoid feeding your hens.

No tomato leaves, no rhubarb stalks or leaves, no eggplant leaves.

No Avocado in any form. No apple seeds or raw dried beans. No chocolate, coffee beans or tea-bags.

Nothing moldy like old stale bread etc, including moldy fruit or vegetables.

No citrus fruits or dairy products such as milk, cheese, yogurt etc.

Nothing sweet - including chocolate!

White rice and pasta have little nutritional value and should be avoided also except as the odd treat perhaps.

It is worth saying that none of the above products will kill your animal should you accidently feed them to your birds, so do not worry on the odd occasion it happens.

However feeding these products long term will be detrimental to the birds health – and your egg production!

Processing Chickens for Meat:

If you are keeping your chickens for eggs only, and are perhaps averse to killing animals, then you should maybe skip this section!

If however your are not squeamish about this natural process, and intend to kill and prepare your birds for the table, then this section will highlight what needs to be done.

If you have been rearing your chickens (or capons) just for the meat aspect alone, then your birds are usually ready for killing at between 7-9 weeks depending on the breed.

If you are killing laying chickens who have past their prime, then this is usually between 3-4 years. They will of course lay a little longer but egg numbers decline rapidly after this time.

Dispatching the Chicken:

Killing any animal has to be done cleanly and effectively, with minimum distress to the animal and in accordance with your own local laws regarding such practice.

My father was an absolute expert, and could break the neck of a chicken in a second by simply holding it by the feet and pulling sharply where the neck joins the head of the bird.

He would then just hang the bird upside down from a branch, and let the blood drain into the head and neck without cutting the throat at all – it was far too messy and needless in his opinion!

Most books on the subject however insist that the bird must be bled properly by cutting the throat, so that you get more clean white flesh from the prepared bird.

With that in mind, the simplest way of achieving this is to get a 'killing cone' (a traffic cone with the end cut off will suffice) and hang it above a receptacle to collect the blood.

Drop the bird head-first down into the cone, and holding it firmly by the back of the head, make a sharp cut across the throat deep enough to slice the artery.

The chicken will quickly bleed-out and expire with minimum distress caused.

Removing The Feathers:

There are two basic ways to remove feathers from the chicken, and that is to pluck them from the bird direct, or to simply skin the bird.

Skinning is the quickest method, although it does leave you without the benefit of cooking a bird with a nice crispy skin!

However it has the advantage of allowing you to prepare your own coating and cook the chicken piece without the skin – which is not to everyone's taste anyway.

Plucking Your Chicken:
The quickest way to remove the feathers from the bird is to heat a large pot of water to about 150 degrees F, then dunk it in the hot water holding by the feet for 2-3 minutes. This will loosen the feathers which are then easily removed by stripping them out by hand.

This is done by gripping handfuls of feathers and pulling in the opposite direction to that which they are growing. Care should be taken to avoid tearing the flesh of the bird.

The larger tail feathers or wing feathers are pulled out directly with a sharp tug.

Skinning the Chicken:
Skinning as a way of removing feathers is simply a matter of chopping the head, wings, and feet off the bird; then beginning at the neck, insert a sharp knife between the skin and the flesh and ease your way down the breast.

The skin on the back will put up a little more resistance, but continue with the knife then insert your fingers between the skin and the breast and pull away the skin as you travel down the bird.

As you get down to the thighs simply continue down the legs and then the wings, until the whole skin is able to be pulled away from the bird.

It sounds a bit complicated but it is one of these tasks that once you have done it for a first time, it becomes easier and easier with practice. Certainly unless your are trying to keep the skin whole for some reason, then there is no need to worry about making a mess of it.

Cleaning & Dressing The Bird:

To remove the chicken guts, slip the knife into the area just below the vent and slice from side to side as in the picture.

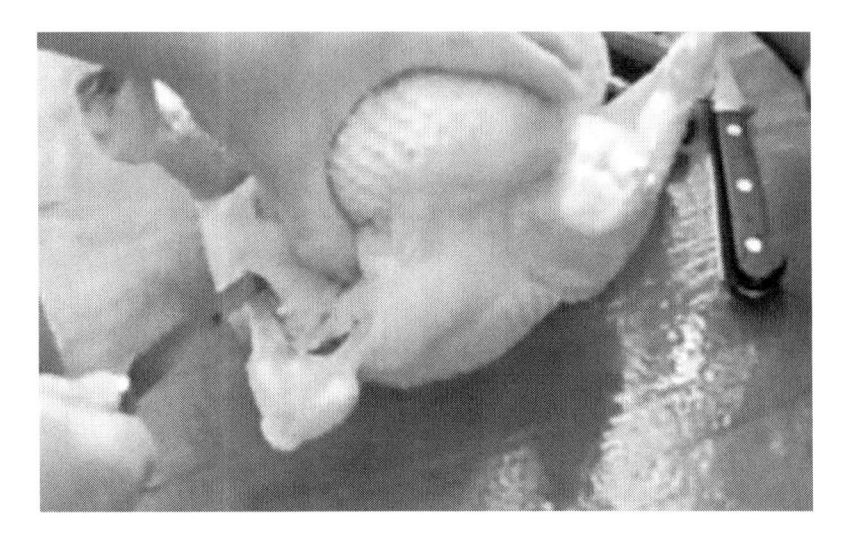

When this is done, cut up each side to leave a hole large enough for you to slip your hand up inside the chest cavity and pull out the chicken innards, this will require some effort. Be careful not to burst the gall bladder in particular as this could taint the meat.

Once that is done and you have made sure everything is removed, turn the bird over onto its chest as per the picture below.

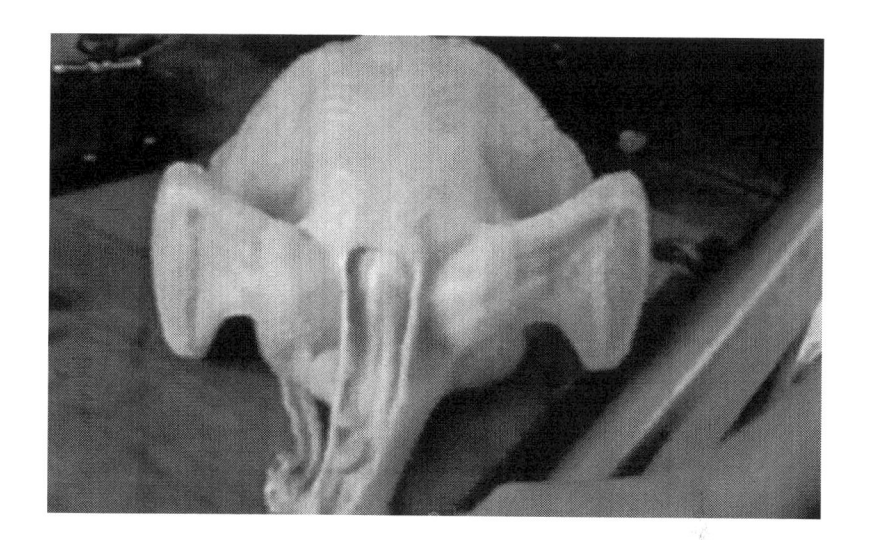

Go to the neck area and cut in to expose the neck itself, then remove the neck with strong shears.

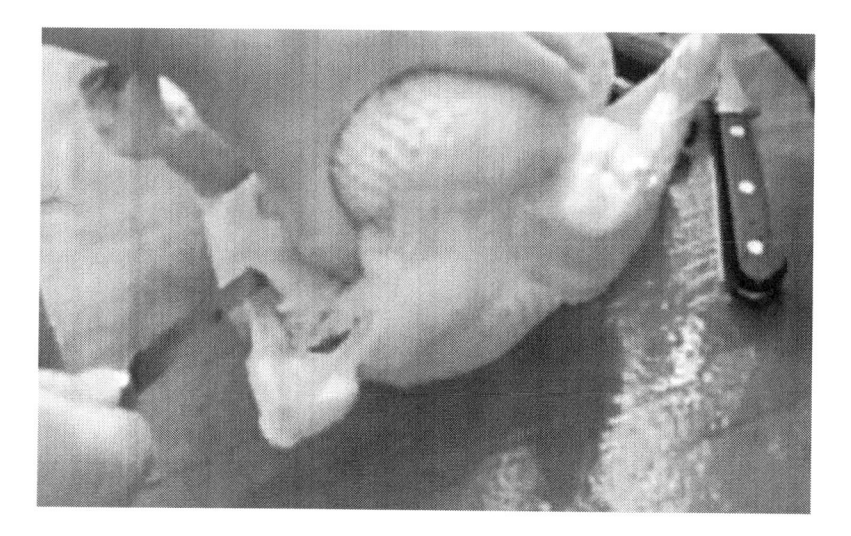

Remove the neck then find and remove the crop by cutting away the membrane that connects it to the bird. The crop is usually quite obvious as it is often quite full with the birds recent meal.

Turn the bird over again and trim away the loose flesh around the neck.

Remove the legs by breaking the bone at the knee and slipping the knife between the joint to remove the leg. The wings can be removed the same way or by cutting them off with heavy shears.

Check out the chest cavity once more to be sure that everything is removed, then thoroughly rise it through with a hose or straight under the tap.

***

Tasty Chicken Recipes!

Please try out this selection of 10 tasty chicken recipes courtesy of F. A. Paris kindle book 'Fantastic Chicken' (copied with permission).

This is a selection of dishes that I particularly like, however you can see the rest of the recipes offered by clicking on the link above – which in case you are wondering, is Not an affiliate link.

Chicken Breast With Parma Ham, Honey & Herbs

(Serves 4)

Ingredients:

- 4 chicken breasts
- 8 strips Parma ham or thin bacon
- 2 table spoons mixed dry herbs
- 2 table spoons runny honey
- 2 table spoons olive oil
- 2 tsp of sea salt

Preparation:

Clean the chicken breasts, then dry with some absorbent kitchen paper.
Wrap two pieces of Parma ham around each chicken breast and place on an oven-proof tray.

Mix the olive oil and the honey together in a suitable container, then brush liberally over the chicken. Sprinkle with the dry herbs, to give a good coating. Season with the Sea Salt.

Place in a hot oven at 180f for 25 minutes.

Best served sliced diagonally, and placed on a bed of Basmati rice.

*****

Spicy Chicken Casserole (2)
(Serves 4-6)

Ingredients:

- 1 ½ lb (680g) diced chicken
- 1 pint (0.45 ltr) chicken stock
- 2 hot chillies (chopped fine)
- 2 onions (chopped)
- 2 cloves garlic (crushed)
- 2 peppers (1 red 1 yellow chopped)
- 1 table spoon tomato paste
- 1 table spoon tomato ketchup
- 6 baby sweet corn (chopped)
- ¼ lb (113g) sliced mushrooms
- 1 table spoon orange marmalade
- Salt & pepper to taste.

Preparation:

Place all the ingredients (minus the stock) into a suitably sized casserole dish, and mix thoroughly adding seasoning.

Pour in the chicken stock, then place in a pre-heated oven set at 180C for 1.5 hours.

Add thickening agent (cornflower or arrowroot) and cook for a further 5-10 mins.

Season as required and serve with traditional vegetables or boiled rice.

*****

Honey Glazed Roast Chicken
(Serves 4-6)

Ingredients:

- 3 ½ lb (1.58 kg) Chicken
- 3 tablespoons runny honey
- 2 table spoons extra virgin olive oil
- 1 tsp balsamic vinegar
- 1 tsp soy sauce
- 1 tsp paprika
- Sea-Salt & pepper to season

Preparation:

After the chicken is cleaned and prepared with any giblets removed; place the whole bird on a suitable oven tray.

Mix the olive oil, honey, paprika and other ingredients together, then brush over the chicken. (use around half of the mix)

Add to a pre-heated oven at 180C and cook for approx 30 minutes, then carefully remove from oven and brush over the rest of the mix. Season with the Sea-salt and ground black pepper.

Add to the oven and cook for a further 60 minutes. Test and see that the juice runs clear when the bird is pierced at the thickest parts.

After skimming away the excess fat, mix the juice in the oven tray with some chicken granules or other thickener to make a delicious gravy.

Carve and serve with roast potatoes and vegetables, placing sauce in a gravy boat for pouring – delicious!

*****

Jamaican Jerk Chicken
(Serves 6)

Ingredients:

- 12 chicken drumsticks
- 2 table spoons sunflower oil
- 2 tsp allspice
- 1 tsp cinnamon
- 2 hot chillies
- 1 table spoon runny honey
- 1 table spoon soy sauce
- Salt & pepper to season.

Preparation:

Add all the ingredients less the chicken into a food processor, and grind down to a fine paste.

Cut the chicken drumsticks in several places, leaving deep scores, then liberally rub in the spice mix.

Place in a hot oven at 190C, or place on a barbeque and cook for approx 20 minutes, turning several times during cooking.

Test and see that the juice runs clear, and that the flesh is no longer pink on the inside. (especially if barbequing!)

Fantastic finger food when served with a crusty loaf and a cold beer!

*****

Chicken & Smoked Ham Stew
(Serves 4-6)

Ingredients:

- 8 oz (226g) smoked ham (cubed)
- 1 ½ lb (680g) chicken (cubed)
- 6-8 scallops
- 2 pints (0.94 ltr) chicken stock
- 2 hot chilli's (fine sliced)
- 2 table spoons vegetable oil
- 1 tsp turmeric
- 2 tsp chopped parsley
- 2 tsp chopped thyme or rosemary
- 1 large onion (Diced)
- 2 sticks celery (chopped)
- 1 garlic clove
- 1 - 14 oz tin of chopped tomatoes
- 2 red peppers (chopped)
- 1 table spoon tomato relish
- Salt & pepper to season

Preparation:

Heat the oil in a saucepan and add the onion, red peppers and garlic. Fry for 3-4 minutes then add the chicken and fry for a further 4-5 minutes.

Add the stock and all the other ingredients. Season to flavour: and cover with a lid. Cook over a gentle heat for 45 minutes.

Taste, then season to suit if required.

Best served on a bed of rice with a garnish of chopped parsley.

*****

Spatchcocked Chicken Stew
(Serves 2-4)

Ingredients:

- 1 Small Chicken (cleaned and spatchcocked-(split in half)
- 8 shallots (whole)
- 2 red or yellow peppers (sliced)
- 1 clove garlic (crushed)
- 1 table spoon butter
- 1 table spoon olive oil
- 2 potatoes (diced small)
- 1 – 14 oz tin chopped tomatoes
- ½ pint chicken stock
- 1 glass red wine
- Salt & pepper

Preparation:

Heat the oil and butter in a large sauce pan, then add the spatchcocked chicken, turning frequently until all sides are browned.

Once this is done, then pour away excess fat, leaving just a little and add the shallots, potatoes and garlic. Fry for a further 4-5 mins before adding the peppers, chopped tomatoes, wine and stock. Season with salt & pepper. Cover with a lid and simmer for 45 minutes.

Serve on a bed of steamed rice.

*****

Fried Chicken With Lemon & Ginger
(Serves 4)

Ingredients:

- 4 chicken drumsticks (skinned)
- 4 chicken thighs (skinned)
- 3 table spoons virgin olive oil
- 4 oz (113g) plain flour
- 1 tsp paprika
- 2 tsp dried ginger
- 1 lemon (juiced and grated)
- 1 table honey
- 1 tsp chilli flakes
- Salt & crushed black pepper to taste

Preparation:

Add the olive oil to a container along with the lemon juice, chilli flakes, honey, salt & pepper and mix thoroughly.
Put the flour into a container and add the paprika, and dried ginger and season with salt & pepper.
Coat the chicken with the marinade, then dip into the flour mix before setting in the fridge for 60 minutes. Re-coat with

the flour then place into a hot pan and brown for 10-15 minutes on a high heat.

Place into a hot oven (250c) on a baking tray and cook for a further 30 minutes.

*****

Spicy Chicken Burgers
(Serves 4-6)

Ingredients:

- 1 lb (453g) ground (minced) chicken
- 1 small onion (fine diced)
- 2 tsp chilli flakes
- 1 tsp paprika
- 1 tsp mixed dried herbs
- 1 table spoon tomato ketchup
- 4 oz (113g) breadcrumbs
- 1 egg (beaten)
- Salt & pepper to season

Preparation:

Lightly fry the onion in a pan for 2-3 minutes to soften. Remove and place in a mixing bowl with the other ingredients.

Mix thoroughly then form into patties about ½ inch (10mm) thick.

Fry evenly on each side for 5-10 minutes.

Serve in buns or on a bed of crispy lettuce with a tomato relish.

*****

Traditional Coq au Vin
(Serves 4)

Ingredients:

- 4 chicken thighs
- 4 chicken drumsticks
- 6 oz (170g) Smokey bacon (rind less, chopped)
- 1 bouquet garni
- 6 oz small button mushrooms
- 1 doz shallots or small onions
- 2 table spoons rapeseed oil
- 1 table spoon butter
- 2 garlic cloves
- ¾ pint (0.34 ltr) red wine
- 3 table spoons brandy
- 2 tsp dried mixed herbs
- Salt & pepper to season

Preparation:

Heat the oil and butter in a saucepan and fry the chicken pieces for 5-10 minutes until golden brown. Remove from pan and add the bacon, frying for 4-5 minutes then adding the onion, garlic and mushrooms.

Fry for a further 5 minutes, then add the chicken pieces. Heat the Brandy or Cognac in a saucepan, carefully set alight and pour over the chicken pieces.

When the flaming has subsided then add the wine, bouquet garni, herbs and simmer for a further 40 minutes.

Thicken sauce if needed with a little cornflower, cooking for a further 5 minutes.

Best served with a buttery mashed potato and vegetables.

*****

Herby Chicken Breasts Stuffed With Cream Cheese & Prunes

(Serves 4)

Ingredients:

- 4 Chicken breasts
- 4 table spoons cream cheese
- 4 table spoons chopped seeded prunes
- 4 tsp mixed dry herbs
- 4 table spoons runny honey
- Sea salt & pepper seasoning

Preparation:

Mix the cream cheese and the finely chopped prunes together in a suitable dish.

Carefully flatten out the chicken breasts to about ½ and inch (10mm), with the use of a kitchen roller; season with salt & pepper then lay out on an oiled oven dish.

Spoon the mixture into the centre of the chicken and pull together with cocktail sticks or twine to hold in place.
Brush over the honey and sprinkle with the mixed herbs.
Season with salt & pepper.
Cook in a hot oven (250C) for 35 minutes.

Excellent serve with boiled potatoes and vegetables – even better with a cheese sauce!

*****

Authors Note:

Finally I would like to say THANKS A LOT for purchasing my book. I do hope that you have found it helpful and informative – and you enjoy the chicken recipes from F.A.Paris's book!

Also, If you can spare the time I would much appreciate your thoughts on the amazon review page.

You can check out the other books I have on Homesteading Animals at these links below.

***

Books In The Homesteading Series:

Homesteading Animals – Rearing Rabbits (book 1)

Homesteading Animals – Delightful Ducks (book 2)

Homesteading Animals: Gourmet Geese (book 3)

Homesteading Animals: Raising Chickens (book 4)

Made in the USA
Lexington, KY
22 June 2015